Searchlight BOOKS™

Saving Animals with Science

Wildlife Crossings

Lisa Idzikowski

Lerner Publications ◆ Minneapolis

For my family

Lerner Publications Company
An imprint of Lerner Publishing Group, Inc.
241 First Avenue North
Minneapolis, MN 55401 USA

For reading levels and more information, look up this title at www.lernerbooks.com.

Main body text set in Adrianna Regular.
Typeface provided by Chank.

Editor: Annie Zheng **Photo Editor:** Annie Zheng

Library of Congress Cataloging-in-Publication Data

Names: Idzikowski, Lisa, author.
Title: Wildlife crossings / Lisa Idzikowski.
Description: Minneapolis : Lerner Publications, [2024] | Series: Searchlight books - saving animals with science | Includes bibliographical references and index. | Audience: Ages 8–11 | Audience: Grades 4–6 | Summary: "Have you ever tried to help a salamander cross a busy street? Researchers are making it easier for all animals to cross safely! Readers learn how wildlife crossings are connecting animals and their habitats"— Provided by publisher.
Identifiers: LCCN 2023013882 (print) | LCCN 2023013883 (ebook) | ISBN 9798765609170 (library binding) | ISBN 9798765624821 (paperback) | ISBN 9798765617380 (epub)
Subjects: LCSH: Wildlife crossings—Juvenile literature. | BISAC: JUVENILE NONFICTION / Animals / Animal Welfare
Classification: LCC SK356.W54 I39 2024 (print) | LCC SK356.W54 (ebook) | DDC 333.95/4—dc23/eng/20230512

LC record available at https://lccn.loc.gov/2023013882
LC ebook record available at https://lccn.loc.gov/2023013883

Manufactured in the United States of America
1-1009626-51595-6/7/2023

Table of Contents

Chapter 1

ANIMALS IN MOTION

Snakes slither, salamanders crawl, and bison wander. Every year, millions of animals travel due to food, mating, and seasonal changes. But as vehicles became more common, people began building roads. When roads cut off animal pathways or their habitats, animals are forced to cross busy highways and must dodge speeding cars and trucks.

Unfortunately, not all animals get across safely. In the US, over a million road accidents every year involve hitting an animal. But wildlife crossings are helping more animals cross safely.

Wildlife Crossings

Wildlife crossings are special structures that help animals cross human-made barriers without getting hurt.

AN ELK WAITING TO CROSS THE ROAD

An overpass in the Netherlands

A wildlife crossing that goes over a road is an overpass. One that goes under a road is an underpass. These bridges can even go around streets and highways. Wildlife crossings provide open pathways for animals all around the world.

Deep Dive

Bison Bridge

Some people think the old I-80 bridge over the Mississippi River should be torn down. But not conservationist Chad Pregracke. He imagines it as a home for bison to roam. If he gets his wish, this span of bridge between Iowa and Illinois will become home to a small herd of eight to ten bison. This "Bison Bridge" would be the longest human-made wildlife crossing in the world.

Pregracke is part of an organization that hopes to repurpose the I-80 bridge (*right*) into a wildlife crossing.

Chapter 2

FURRY FREEWAYS

Discover how wildlife crossings help furry creatures, such as koalas and big cats, cross freeways around the world!

Koala Crossing

Koalas often spend their days in trees, but at night they move along the ground. This has led to accidents on the road when koalas try to cross. Scientists in Queensland, Australia, found a way to help by adding walkways to existing drainage tunnels—structures that pass under roadways and drain water. To observe how well these crossings worked, researchers tagged and tracked seventy-two koalas. Over thirty months, 130 koalas were seen using these crossings. Road deaths dropped significantly near these crossings.

In some parts of Australia, koalas are endangered. Wildlife crossings help lower their death rate.

Cat Walks

Florida panthers are large, wild cats found in southern parts of Florida. They are on the endangered species list. At one point, no more than thirty Florida panthers lived in the wild. Road accidents are one of the biggest threats to Florida panthers.

To counter these accidents, Florida began planning wildlife crossings on Interstate 75 in 1972. This move provided 100-foot-long (30 m) crossings and 40 feet (12 m) of total land along drainage tunnels under the highway.

A Florida panther attempting to cross a busy highway

An overpass crossing Interstate 75 in Florida

By the 1990s, the state had built twenty-four wildlife crossings and updated twelve bridges for Florida panthers. Many Florida panthers use these crossings to get from one side of the highway to the other.

Bridges for Bears

Banff National Park is one of Canada's oldest national parks. It is home to bears, elk, deer, and more. But as park visitors increase, so does road traffic. That means there's a higher chance of animals getting hurt.

In 1996, Banff National Park built its first two wildlife overpasses. These cement bridges arch over the highway. To a person standing underneath one of these bridges, it looks like concrete. But to someone standing on top of it, it's a forest that connects one side of the park to the other.

Banff National Park is home to many animals, including bighorn sheep.

Cars pass underneath overpasses at Banff National Park, while animals safely cross above them.

Since these overpasses were built, Banff National Park has built more overpasses and underpasses. Wildlife crossing researchers have found that grizzly bears, elk, and deer are drawn to using big, open structures, such as overpasses. Meanwhile, cougars and black bears tend to use small, covered crossings, such as underpasses.

Mountain Lions in the City

Los Angeles, California, is famous for its mountain lions. These big cats live near the city in the Santa Monica Mountains. Every year, several mountain lions get hit and killed by cars. Busy freeways also separate them from other habitats and mountain lions, since they're unable to cross. This is called fragmentation. Scientists fear these LA mountain lions will one day become extinct.

A mountain lion standing on a tree branch

The Wallis Annenberg Wildlife Crossing project began construction in 2022.

A new highway bridge could prevent that. The Wallis Annenberg Wildlife Crossing project plans to provide safe passage for these mountain lions from the Santa Monica Mountains to the nearby Santa Susana Mountains. The crossing will be the largest in the world at 210 feet (64 m) long and roughly 175 feet (53 m) wide. The top of the crossing will be filled with plants native to the area. The crossing will rise above a busy, ten-lane highway underneath. As thousands of cars speed along, mountain lions and other wildlife will safely march overhead.

Chapter 3

HOOVED HIGHWAYS

Discover how nature's hooved animals, such as deer and pronghorns, are making their crossings safely!

Green Wave

Every year, thousands of elk, pronghorns, deer, and bighorn sheep make seasonal journeys. In the fall, these animals migrate south to avoid snow and cold. In the spring, they return north once plants begin to grow and turn green. Scientists call this riding the green wave.

Elk migrating in Grand Teton National Park, Wyoming

But every spring and fall, some of these migrating, hooved animals get hit by vehicles on roads. Some animals have even had trouble crossing fences. That's why people have started building wildlife crossings that animals can use to migrate.

Spotlight On

Deer 255

Deer 255 is a female mule deer living in the region between Wyoming and Idaho. She wears a tan, leather collar that allows researchers to track her movements. Each spring, Deer 255 travels from the Red Desert to Grand Teton National Park in Wyoming. That's about 240 miles (386 km)! Her migration is one of the longest known of all North American hooved animals.

A female mule deer

ONE OF THE TWO OVERPASSES CROSSING US 191 IN WYOMING

Pronghorn Path

Pronghorns are migratory animals. Every spring, they can be spotted migrating north from western Wyoming. In 2012, the state completed six underpasses and two overpasses on US 191. The two overpasses are 40 feet (12 m) tall and covered with soil and grass. They are located 6.5 miles (10.5 km) apart. Pronghorns walk over the bridge as cars drive on the busy road below.

A herd of bison crossing the Madison River in Yellowstone National Park

Breaking Barriers for Bison

In 2022, thirteen American bison were killed while crossing US 191 in Montana. Crossing this strip of highway can be deadly for other animals too, including elk, grizzly bears, and wolves. Conservationists are working to get the world's first buffalo wildlife bridge built. If approved, an overpass would be built at Madison River crossing over US 191. Fencing would be added along the highway to herd animals toward the crossing and away from the road.

Spotlight On

President Joe Biden

On November 15, 2021, President Joe Biden signed the Infrastructure Investment and Jobs Act. This bill will provide over a trillion dollars for fixing roads, bridges, water pipes, and power grids. Roughly one thousand wildlife crossings exist in the US. Over $300 million from this bill will be used to build more wildlife crossings all over the country.

Biden signing the Infrastructure Investment and Jobs Act

Chapter 4

SLIPPERY AND SWAMPY

Wildlife crossings help keep animals safe as they cross busy roads. But not all these animals are big, furry, or hooved. Discover how wildlife crossings are helping salamanders, snakes, and more!

Frogs and Salamanders

On certain spring nights in Vermont, people gather and gear up for a rescue mission. They help frogs and salamanders cross the road. In some towns, more

Volunteers wear safety clothes that reflect light at night as they help small animals, such as salamanders, cross the road.

than five hundred people volunteer on these nights.

Cars can do a lot of damage to small animals, especially frogs and salamanders. In Salisbury, people carry the animals across in their hands, so the animals don't get hit. Some towns even close a part of the road every year so volunteers can move the animals safely. An amphibian crossing would make protecting amphibians easier.

Monkton, Vermont, has such a crossing. In 2016, the town finished building two amphibian underpasses under Monkton-Vergennes Road. These concrete tunnels have a natural bottom with soil and plants. Fencing keeps amphibians, such as frogs and salamanders, from getting onto the road. Since the project's completion, over two thousand amphibians have been spotted using the tunnels to cross the road.

Underpasses such as this one have fencing that guides amphibians inside.

A fox snake attempting to cross the road

Slithering Snakes

Wildlife crossings are not just for amphibians or large mammals. Snakes also benefit from these crossings. In Windsor, Ontario, Highway 401 is a big barrier for fox snakes to cross. The road divides the fox snake's habitat. When snakes try to cross the busy road, they sometimes get hurt. In response, the city built a wildlife crossing over the highway. Fox snakes, deer, and even coyotes use the crossing.

Crab Crossing

Every year in October or November, Australia's Christmas Island comes alive. Millions of Christmas Island red crabs migrate across the island. An estimated forty to fifty million crabs make the journey every year to mate.

A national park staff member watching the annual Christmas Island red crab migration

This bridge is a special structure made just for crabs.

But cars pose a danger to these crabs. So the community closes roads when the migration begins. In some areas on the island, underpasses beneath roads guide crabs to safety. But on the busiest highway, Christmas Island rangers built something special. A crab bridge 16 feet (5 m) tall rises over this street. It's made from mesh, a material that uses metal wire or thread. Crabs grip the mesh and scurry safely over the bridge.

Building Bridges

Wildlife crossings are becoming more common. Whether it's an underpass or an overpass, wildlife crossings help animals cross more safely than ever before. Scientists and engineers will continue to improve these structures to protect more of the world's wild creatures.

An underpass beneath a highway

Save the Day

In the United States, many people rely on driving as a main form of transportation. But during the COVID-19 pandemic stay-at-home orders in March and April of 2020, road accidents involving wild animals dropped by as much as 50 percent in some states. Fewer cars on the roads would lessen their impact on wildlife. What solution would you come up with to help lower animal accidents on the road?

Glossary

conservationist: a person who acts for the protection of the environment and wildlife

drainage tunnel: a tunnel to drain water

endangered: at risk of extinction

extinct: no longer existing

fragmentation: when an animal's habitat is interrupted, such as by a road

habitat: the place where a plant or animal naturally lives

migrate: to move from one place to another in a regular pattern

overpass: a wildlife crossing that goes over a road or highway

pronghorn: a fast-moving animal that looks like an antelope

underpass: a wildlife crossing that goes under a road or highway

Learn More

Duffield, Katy. *Crossings*. New York: Beach Lane Books, 2020.

Interesting Engineering: "29 of the Most Heartwarming Wildlife Crossings Around the World"
https://interestingengineering.com/culture/29-of-the-most-heartwarming-wildlife-crossings-around-the-world

Mattern, Joanne. *Caution: Turtles and Frogs Ahead!* Egremont, MA: Red Chair, 2023.

National Geographic Society: Wildlife Crossings
https://education.nationalgeographic.org/resource/wildlife-crossings/

Smithsonian: Video of Christmas Crab Migration
https://ocean.si.edu/ocean-life/invertebrates/video-christmas-crab-migration

Walker, Tracy Sue. *Wildlife Conservation Technology*. Minneapolis: Lerner Publications, 2024.

Index

Photo Acknowledgments

Image credits: Manuel Romaris/Moment/Getty Images, p. 5; Artur Debat/Moment/Getty Images, p. 6; Justin Wilkens/Shutterstock, p 7; Laura Howden/500px/Getty Images, p. 9; Michael A. Damanski/Shutterstock, p. 10; Michael Warren/iStock/Getty Images, p. 11; Mark Newman/The Image Bank/Getty Images, p. 12; Craig Zerbe/iStock/Getty Images, p. 13; Max Allen/Alamy, p. 14; AP Photo/Marcio Jose Sanchez, p. 15; Kino Alyse/Moment/Getty Images, p. 17; Pierre Longnus/The Image Bank/Getty Images, p. 18; William Campbell/Corbis News/Getty Images, p. 19; Lee Rentz/Alamy, p. 20; World Politics Archive (WPA)/Alamy, p. 21; AP Photo/Kristopher Radder, p. 23; YueStock/Shutterstock, p. 24; Mike Wilhelm/Shutterstock, p. 25; Xinhua/Alamy, p. 26; neil bowman/iStock/Getty Images, p. 27; Rudmer Zwerver/Shutterstock, p. 28.

Cover: Jorg Greuel/Photodisc/Getty Images.